THE B

JAMES

A BIBLE STUDY GUIDE

THE BOOK OF
JAMES
A BIBLE STUDY GUIDE

VINCE MILLER

EQUIP PRESS

Colorado Springs

THE BOOK OF
JAMES

Published by Equip Press, Colorado Springs, CO

Scripture quotations marked (ESV) are taken from The ESV® Bible (The Holy Bible, English Standard Version®) copyright © 2001 by Crossway, a publishing ministry of Good News Publishers. ESV® Text Edition: 2011. The ESV® text has been reproduced in cooperation with and by permission of Good News Publishers.
Unauthorized reproduction of this publication is prohibited. Used by permission.
All rights reserved.

Scripture quotations marked (KJV) are taken from the King James Bible. Accessed on Bible Gateway at www.BibleGateway.com.

Scripture quotations marked (NASB) are taken from the New American Standard Bible® (NASB), copyright © 1960, 1962, 1963, 1968, 1971, 1972, 1973, 1975, 1977, 1995 by The Lockman Foundation, www.Lockman.org. Used by permission.

Scripture quotations marked (NIV) are taken from the Holy Bible, New International Version. Copyright © 1973, 1978, 1984, 2011 by Biblica, Inc.® Used by permission. All rights reserved worldwide.

Scripture quotations marked (NKJV) are taken from the New King James Version®. Copyright © 1982 by Thomas Nelson, Inc. Used by permission. All rights reserved.

Scripture quotations marked (NLT) are taken from the Holy Bible, New Living Translation, copyright © 1996, 2004, 2015 by Tyndale House Foundation. Used by permission of Tyndale House Publishers, Inc., Carol Stream, Illinois 60188. All rights reserved.

Scripture quotations marked (NRSV) are taken from the New Revised Standard Version Bible, copyright © 1989 the Division of Christian Education of the National Council of the Churches of Christ in the United States of America. Used by permission. All rights reserved.

First Edition: 2021
The Book of James / Vince Miller
Paperback ISBN: 978-1-951304-62-1
eBook ISBN: 978-1-951304-63-8

EQUIP PRESS
Colorado Springs

CONTENTS

HOW TO USE THIS HANDBOOK

VIDEOS FOR THIS HANDBOOK

As you navigate this handbook, you will discover that the lessons are designed for use with online videos. These videos are viewable with a membership at our website: **www.beresolute. org**. You can use the videos for individual growth or with a group. Each lesson corresponds with the video of the same title. The best part is Vince Miller has structured the videos to provide relevant content for reflection and discussion so that you don't need hours to prepare. He does the work for you. Just push *play* on the video, and then reference this handbook.

THE METHOD

We believe in providing you with a full-scale game plan for growth. We are not just giving you content, but a *method* that has been field-tested with hundreds of thousands. While choosing the material is essential, we believe our step-by-step process is one of the best for producing a spiritual change. We have tested the components in each session and how they link together within a series or group of series that complement ongoing growth. Our goal is to produce life change. In each lesson, you will notice clear goals and outcomes, purposeful reflection and discussion questions, a rich study of God's Word, and practical application with actionable steps to be taken. While we know you need content, we hope our commitment to this method deepens their relationship with Christ and with one another.

THERE IS MORE IN THIS SERIES

Remember, once you finish this series there are many others that follow it and build upon it. Don't do just one series, do them all!

HOW TO LEAD A GROUP

ONE | GATHER YOUR TEAM

Assembling a team is critical. A team should include a pair of leaders who become the *"On-Site Hosts"* for the experience. We believe working in pairs is by far the most practical approach. Remember, every pilot needs a wingman.

TWO | RECRUIT PARTICIPANTS

Don't stress: whether you recruit half a dozen or a hundred, the content will be useful. We have found the best recruiting success comes from finding people who are hungry to grow spiritually. While the content is suitable for any believer of any age, the best recruit is the one who wants to be there, someone who hungers for the Word of God, and occasionally some food as well!

THREE | MAKE SURE EACH PARTICIPANT HAS A HANDBOOK

Our guides may be purchased in the online store: www. beresolute.org. These are your guides for taking notes, guiding a dialogue in your group, and recording outcomes at the end of every lesson. Handbooks also include other materials for additional development. You will want one for each lesson series.

FOUR | ONLINE RESOURCES FOR LEADERS

If you have purchased online video access with your membership, you can view all the material. You will be able to listen to audio recaps, watch the videos, read the full transcripts, and even review past lessons. There are also training articles and videos online to help you lead your group.

FIVE | MORE MATERIAL & VINCE MILLER

At Resolute, we are not just providing content. We are inviting you to an experience. Here are other tools you can utilize.

- Need a devotional? Read the Daily Devotional: www. beresolute.org/mdd
- Need prayer? Vince Miller will personally pray for you: www.beresolute.org
- Need a speaker? Invite Vince Miller to speak: beresolute.org/vince-miller
- Need help as a leader? Contact Vince Miller directly at vince@beresolute.org

It is our goal to partner with you and your ministry. We want to resource you with tools that compliment your development as a follower and a leader.

SIX | CONNECT SOCIALLY

We would love to have you join our social networks. Head to our home page and connect with us on Twitter, LinkedIn, and Facebook.

JAMES

ABOUT VINCE MILLER

Vince Miller was born in Vallejo, California, and grew up on the West Coast. At twenty, he made a profession of faith while in college and felt a strong, sudden call to work in full-time ministry. After college and graduate school, he invested two decades working with notable ministries like Young Life, InterVarsity Christian Fellowship, the local church, and in senior interim roles. He currently lives in St. Paul, Minnesota, with his wife Christina and their three teenage children.

In March 2014, he founded Resolute out of his passion for discipleship and leadership development of men. This passion was born out of his personal need for growth. Vince turned everywhere to find a man who would mentor, disciple, and develop him throughout his spiritual life. He often received two answers from well-meaning Christian leaders: *either they did not know what to do in a mentoring relationship, or they simply did not have the time to do it.* Vince learned that he was not alone. Many Christian men were seeking this type of mentorship relationship. Therefore, he felt compelled to build an organization that would focus on two things: ensuring that men who want to be discipled have the opportunity and that they have real tools to disciple other men.

Vince is an authentic and transparent leader who loves to communicate with men and has a deep passion for God's Word. He has authored several books, and he is the primary content creator of all Resolute content and training materials.

A PERSONAL NOTE FROM VINCE

I pray this experience will benefit your life and your spiritual journey. I hope you will do three things as you engage. First, that you will be receptive to the Word of God. I love that we dig into the Bible each time we meet. At Resolute, the Bible is not an afterthought. It is the means of discovering God and transformation. Second, lean into the community of this experience. Build friendships, share transparently, and have conversations that go beyond the superficial. Third, apply what you have learned. Take an action item with you every week, knowing that one small step weekly leads to success over a lifetime.

Keep moving forward,

INTRODUCTION

James's letter is not written to people living in ease, peace, and comfort. It's quite the opposite. From the first words it challenges a reader. It was a letter intended for believers with a Jewish background dispersed into house churches across the countryside. They were believers who were living in poverty and persecution. However, it doesn't have that soft edge you think it would have to a struggling people. Instead, it coaches and challenges a reader to rise to the call of the present challenges.

The letter is written by a man named James. James was the brother of Jesus—or half-brother, that is. Mary, the virgin mother of Jesus, was given a child by God. She was engaged to a man named Joseph. After Jesus was born Mary and Joseph consummated their marriage and gave birth to at least six other children, the exact number we don't know. There were at least four other sons (Joseph, James, Jude, and Simon) and at least two daughters. But not a lot more is known about this family.

In reading Acts chapters 12 & 15, which is the history book of the New Testament, we discover that after Jesus' life, death, and resurrection, James became a leader in the church in Jerusalem along with Peter and the disciples of Jesus. Most of James's ministry focused on Jews who became Christ-followers. James was a leader in the first Christian community, and there were two challenges this community encountered. First, there was a great famine during this time, which affected commerce and increased national poverty. Second, the Jewish converts to Christianity faced a lot of persecution for their new faith by Jewish leaders in Jerusalem. It's in the face of these challenges that James writes a letter to Jewish believers across the Empire.

This letter is a challenging letter and one that will push us to new limits in our faith. In this series, we are going to work through James chapter by chapter. The five sessions and five chapters will address these topics:

- Chapter One: Two Tests of Conviction
- Chapter Two: Living A Consistent Life
- Chapter Three: From Foolish to Wise Talk
- Chapter Four: New Desires Result in New Actions
- Chapter Five: Three Action of Great Followers

I want to encourage you to read through the letter of James in one sitting. You will be able to follow along in this study guide. It also has some daily devotionals that will give you something to reflect on daily. You'll see some opening and closing discussion questions in your handbooks for group discussion that will help you dig into the topic a little more. So grab a Bible, a journal, your handbook, and let's dig into chapter one of this letter from James.

TWO TESTS OF CONVICTION

OPENING QUESTIONS

- Are there certain prerequisites to applying for your current job?
- What do these prerequisites teach you and why are they important?
- What are common tests for Christians today?
- How do they prove we are followers of Christ?

CHAPTER 1

I cannot tell you how many times I have experienced a conviction in my life. Most of these feelings (or moments of conviction) are very private to me. They are moments in which I experience a fragment of thought about an attitude or an action in my life. And in these moments, it seems I hear an almost audible voice that says something of this nature:

"You need to change _____."

"You've put _____ off too long."

"You cannot go on living, acting, and feeling _____."

I don't think I am the only one who has ever heard these voices of conviction. But most of the time when I hear these voices I live in the regret, guilt, and shame of the conviction rather than taking action on them. I allow these useful feelings of regret and guilt to become the only action that follows my conviction, and therefore I *do* nothing to act. I reflect on the issue and consider the work that needs to be done to rectify it, but it overwhelms me, so I do nothing. This is a wrong response to the voice of conviction. I call this the *conviction gap*, the gap between feeling conviction and acting with conviction.

I believe a lot of Christians live stuck in this gap. We feel convicted by our sin, shortcomings, hurts, and hang-ups but feel perplexed about taking the next step. Because we are either confused about taking the next step or see how challenging that next will be—we remain satisfied with only the guilt and shame of the conviction gap. Therefore, we live in perpetual regret, shame, and guilt, privately telling ourselves we are not good enough and live stuck in the penance of an unchanged life.

It does not have to be this way: you can live with real conviction. There are two tests James says the Christian must endure to close this gap. James addresses them both in chapter one. They are the test of **trials** and the test of **integrity**, and he hammers both of them home.

FIRST | THE TEST OF TRIALS

*Count it all joy, my brothers, when you meet trials of
various kinds, for you know that the testing of your faith
produces steadfastness. And let steadfastness have its full
effect, that you may be perfect and complete,
lacking in nothing.*

JAMES 1:2-4

When it comes to trials, I don't think about joy, but James has a much different view of trials. He sees them with unique insight. He sees a unique opportunity. Like an entrepreneur searching for that new vision, or an inventor looking for that new product, or that musician looks for that next great song, he as a teacher perceives a unique opportunity in every trial. It makes way for a character trait that makes Christians strong and complete—steadfastness.

James's perspective on the challenges of life is essential. This is because James perceives something spiritually beneficial in the pain that life brings. He perceives a spiritual reality and, therefore, a spiritual benefit. This viewpoint brings spiritual optimism about challenges. But let's make sure and differentiate this from human optimism. Human optimism is different. It claims to look at something negative and redefine it as positive from a natural perspective. It means to muster a positive outlook on a negative circumstance, hoping that the power of positive thinking will change how we feel, and eventually change the event itself.

However, the joy that James is talking about is much different. It's a joy that is certain. A joy accomplished in Christ. A certain defeat of sin and eternal damnation is accomplished by God's hand, which gives us indescribable joy even during a trial. Therefore, while we may feel or look defeated by circumstances in this life (even things like poverty or persecution) we walk tall, knowing that God has won the victory. We live sure of this reality and not just hoping for it or ignoring it like human optimism attempts to do. We place our faith in something certain, which results in the joyful embrace of trials, and thus we gladly endure in *steadfastness*. And this is not hopeful thinking, positive thinking, or wishful thinking—this is steadfast certainty based on a spiritual reality.

This is the kind of joy and confidence I believe all want. Yet, at times it is hard to come by, especially when life presses in on us.

For example, try telling someone to *"count it joy"* in job loss, marital failure, health challenges, and catastrophic sin, and tell me how that works out. This is the last thing we want to hear. When we encounter trials like this, all we see is the present challenge and the present pain. In these moments it feels like our life is coming undone. Sometimes the pain of this undoing is more real than our faith. We have all encountered this moment, this collision between trials and our faith. When this happens, we start to say things like this to ourselves:

"God, I beg you to please take this trial from me."
"God, why did you let this happen to me?"

In moments like this, I have seen great followers with great faith wane and become fragile and weak. What we were once so confident about in faith becomes brittle. But James suggests something entirely different. That this is the moment of greatest opportunity, for where **the leap of faith is great there's opportunity for greater faith**. What we so easily believed during good times now gives us this remarkable opportunity. It's in moments of trial we need to remember that Jesus's life, death, and resurrection do not change just because we have encountered a trial. And trials may actually bring us closer to his sufferings; they should not drive us farther away from God, but closer to him.

Now our foe would like nothing more than for us to give up on faith in God—but this is not the response of great followers of great faith. Instead, they are *steadfast*. They preach to themselves in the trial because of the benefit on the other side of it. They say things like Job said when he lost everything, including his family, possessions, and cattle.

Then Job arose and tore his robe and shaved his head
and fell on the ground and worshiped. And he said,
"Naked I came from my mother's womb, and naked shall
I return. The Lord gave, and the Lord has taken away;
blessed be the name of the Lord."

JOB 1:20-21

A Christian's joy in trials does not mean that we do not mourn or feel sadness in a trial, but rather that we see every trial twice. Once with our physical eyes and the second time with our spiritual eyes. And when our human desires inform us about a natural and physical reality, we must preach back to it a supernatural and spiritual truth—one that is *steadfast*. And the best part is that in these moments the steadfast follower receives a blessing. Listen to what James promises a little later in this chapter:

Blessed is the man who remains steadfast under trial, for when he has stood the test, he will receive the crown of life, which God has promised to those who love him.

JAMES 1:12

Notice that while we endure with joy, there is also a certain reality and blessing that comes from it. This blessing is only available for those who remain steadfast in the test, for those who see the trials all the way to the end. Actually, the blessings are numerous, but one is the promise that God gives us about what's on the other side of the trial. The other side of the trial presents us with many opportunities and a great witness to the crown of life God has promised.

SECOND | THE TEST OF INTEGRITY

But be doers of the word, and not hearers only, deceiving yourselves. For if anyone is a hearer of the word and not a doer, he is like a man who looks intently at his natural face in a mirror. For he looks at himself and goes away and at once forgets what he was like.

JAMES 1:22-24

No one strives to live a life of self-deception. But what's interesting is that many Christian's do. We live in a conscious state of self-deception when we **know what we need to do** and then **fail to do it**. This was a major concern of Jesus, and an emphasis in many of his teachings. Yet the required activity is pretty basic. It requires only two things: first, exposure to the truth of God's Word. Second, an action that follows which is done from a pure motivation. That's it. Nothing more.

But as happens in life, there is a lot that can happen in the delay between hearing something and acting on it. In the delay we sometimes:

- *We fail to listen.*
- *We fail to comprehend as we listen.*
- *We listen and yet can be confused about what action to take.*
- *We listen but never take the needed action.*

Each of us is guilty of some type of failure to connect our hearing and action. But the imagery James uses to describe this lack of integrity, or integration is quite vivid. When we fail to act, he describes this as looking at something familiar, like yourself in a mirror, and then forgetting what you look like. It's preposterous and unthinkable example. But yet again, James states there is a blessing for the one who lives a life of integrity:

> *But the one who looks into the perfect law, the law of liberty, and perseveres, being no hearer who forgets but a doer who acts, he will be blessed in his doing.*
>
> **JAMES 1:25**

This time, the blessing is in the act of doing. And why? Because the perfect law, God's Word, is right and righteous every time. Therefore the action will be right and righteous. But it must be done! And notice the two small points James makes about how to increase and build our integrity in this perfect law.

ONE | ASSUME GOD'S WORD IS PERFECT

He challenges us to be *"one who looks into the perfect law."* We need to be looking into the perfect law—God's Word.

I cannot emphasize this enough: **God's Word is the last word on all things for Christians**. This means we should be consulting the Bible regularly with every issue and every challenge we encounter. We must be in the book daily.

TWO | REDUCE THE DELAY BETWEEN HEARING AND ACTING

Second, I would decrease the time between hearing and acting. Just get better at doing things, if not everything, immediately. You know, sometimes hesitation gives way to sin. So take those hesitations off the table.

This simple rule of reducing the delay has increased spiritual momentum in my life. The reason being is that I am looking for the connection between a spiritual conviction and what I need to do to act with conviction. And thus, increasing my integration in the test of my integrity. It's actually easy to do—and easy *not* to do.

This is where we began today. We started with trying to find a way to close the conviction gap. We can do so with these two tests—the tests of **trials** and **integrity**. We do it by remaining steadfast and integrating our hearing and doing as followers of God.

So here is your call to action: I want you to choose one point from this lesson and act on it. Live with greater conviction by:

- Remaining steadfast in a trial you are currently facing.
- Investing time integrating your hearing and doing more quickly.

But do me a favor: don't do nothing! Pass the tests and let God be great in you today.

REFLECTION & DISCUSSION QUESTIONS:

- What's a trial you've had to endure lately?
- How are you handling this?
- What could you do to improve how you are handing this?
- What is God teaching you through it?

DEVOTIONALS FOR JAMES 1

IT'S JOY

> *Count it all joy, my brothers, when you meet trials of various kinds, for you know that the testing of your faith produces steadfastness.*
>
> **JAMES 1:2-3**

This is contrary to how we usually think when we encounter trials of various kinds. Joy is not the word I would use to describe them. But a Jesus-follower's manner of thinking differs from others in this life. We look at situations differently. We see them as God would see them—opportunities for testing. These trials have the potential to increase our faith and force us to look at situations from a spiritual perspective, not a natural one. Therefore we should have more endurance and faith, which produces an increase in steadfastness.

Our faith is not a crutch for the weak-minded, but rather it's for those who are willing to become stronger, be tested further, and find joy in moments we meet trials. So be strong today— strong in the faith and count your joy.

ASK THIS: What's the trial you are facing right now?

DO THIS: Find one aspect of joy to count in this trial.

PRAY THIS: God, I pray that you show something beneficial about the present trial that I may not see, so that I can praise you in this storm.

THE STEADFAST EFFECT

And let steadfastness have its full effect, that you may be perfect and complete, lacking in nothing.

JAMES 1:4

There is an effect that comes from faith under trial—it's steadfastness. But notice steadfastness has its own effect, a *"full effect."* Many of us will endure a partial effect but not a full effect. The pain and discomfort of this life scream, *"Turn back!"* But not James. James tells us to push through the obstacles of faith and look beyond the present pain. It's a call to be steadfast so that we will experience something wonderful that we miss if we give up: perfection, and completeness. If you want to lack nothing in faith, then push through with faith and discover the wonder of the steadfast effect.

ASK THIS: What trial are you presently facing that you want to give up on?

DO THIS: Be steadfast in the faith with me.

PRAY THIS: God, this season beckons me to give in and give up. In my weakness make me stronger. In my unbelief, increase my belief. Please give me strength today to be steadfast and therefore complete lacking nothing.

JUST ASK; IT'S YOURS

If any of you lacks wisdom, let him ask God,
who gives generously to all without reproach,
and it will be given him.

JAMES 1:6

I know I lack some things at present. But upon reflection I have realized that I am keeping these needs to myself. They are locked in the confines of my mind, stirring around and creating only concern. Why do I do this? Do I keep them to myself out of shame? Is it embarrassment? Am I scared to ask because I might look stupid or foolish?

Regardless, James says if we lack, we should ask. And not ask just anyone—ask God. The God who owns all things and is the source of everything good and righteous. And here's the best part, God is waiting for us to ask because he wants to give generously. It's important! God does this without reproach, which is the operative phrase here. This means God gives generously to one who asks without an expression of disapproval or disappointment. Wow!

So get to asking, and stop keeping your needs to yourself.

ASK THIS: What do you need to ask God right now?

DO THIS: Ask him, out loud, and right now.

PRAY THIS: God, I need _____.

THE FAITH-ASK

But let him ask in faith, with no doubting,
for the one who doubts is like a wave of the sea
that is driven and tossed by the wind.

JAMES 1:6

There is a way we should ask: in faith. Faith is confidence in the unseen God. Not only what God does but who he is. If we have faith only in what God does or what we expect him to do, is that really faith? But rather, we should place our faith in God regardless of what happens in the high times and low times, so when the waves of life beat upon us, leading to shipwreck or safety, we're anchored into the only thing that really matters—a God who never changes. So let's ask in confident faith untouched by the events and distractions of life.

ASK THIS: Consider one bold request you want to ask God.

DO THIS: Ask in faith.

PRAY THIS: God, I have asked before, but I am going to ask again. This time with confident faith in you, the unchanging God.

STOP DOUBLE-MINDEDNESS

For that person must not suppose that he will receive anything from the Lord; he is a double-minded man, unstable in all his ways.

JAMES 1:7-8

I think what we want is some stability, not *suppose-ability*. But there is a lot of suppose-ability among Christians. We suppose God will respond to us; therefore, we are unstable in what we believe he will do. But remember, Christian faith is anchored in the person of God, not merely what we expect he will do nor what he does. Therefore our stability is based in the Lord and him alone. So when we ask him, we should not suppose he exists but know that he exists and hears, listens, and responds to us. Therefore we should ask confidently in the Lord and be not double-minded about God, regardless of how he might answer or not answer, because our faith is not in what God will do or not do for us, but in the Lord himself. That's not suppose-ability; that's stability.

ASK THIS: What is your confidence in God based on?

DO THIS: Be stable—have faith in the Lord.

PRAY THIS: God, turn my confidences from what you might do to who you are. Make me stable and single-minded. Cancel my duplicity of thinking.

DANGEROUSLY RICH

Let the lowly brother boast in his exaltation, and the rich in his humiliation, because like a flower of the grass he will pass away. For the sun rises with its scorching heat and withers the grass; its flower falls, and its beauty perishes. So also will the rich man fade away in the midst of his pursuits.

JAMES 1:9-11

There's not a person alive who doesn't imagine the boast of being rich. But James says the rich person isn't rich forever, but only a season. Humiliation awaits the rich because, like the flower's beauty, it is passing and perishing. The rich will fall and fade. But not the lowly. He thoughtfully considers his boast because his boasting is in the Lord, not some temporal pursuit.

ASK THIS: Are you boasting?

DO THIS: Boast in the Lord.

PRAY THIS: God, may I never take the riches of your provision for granted. Your provision is better and lasts longer than anything I can provide for myself.

THE DEATH OF GROWING DESIRE

---

*Then, desire when it has conceived gives birth to sin, and
sin when it is fully grown brings forth death.*

JAMES 1:15

Desire is not a static thing in the life of a follower. It grows, much like a human life grows inside the womb of a woman. It starts with a longing that develops until it matures into a decision, action, and routine behavior. But at some point, it is transformed because desire is conceived. But an evil desire does not give birth to life; on the contrary, it brings death. But here's the question: Why do so many go through all that labor to produce something that produces nothing? Sounds like a waste of time and energy to me.

ASK THIS: What evil desires are bringing you death?

DO THIS: Desire what's good and holy.

PRAY THIS: God, kill my evil desires, and simultaneously replace them with holy desires.

JAMES

LIVING A CONSISTENT LIFE

OPENING QUESTIONS

- Why is consistency a valuable attribute?
- How is a follower's consistency tested over time?

CHAPTER 2

When I was a young teen, my grandfather taught me how to golf. And I quickly discovered that consistency was essential to the game. A consistent swing resulted in consistently well-hit shots.

But over time, as most golfers do, I have developed some inconsistent swing patterns that have resulted in consistently poorly hit balls. And rather than address all these bad habits, I do what most casual golfers do; I compensate with small counter adjustments that make for an ugly swing. When playing, I make these small adjustments in my grip, clubface, and my stance, which results in a horrific-looking swing, all for a ball that occasionally lands in the middle of the fairway.

And don't act like you haven't done this!

But listen to this wisdom from golf legend Jack Nicklaus:

> *If there is one thing I have learned during my years as a*
> *professional, it is that the only thing constant about golf*
> *is its inconsistency.*

Now, of course, he's overstating the point. Please remember, I did just quote one of the greatest golfers of all time (if not the greatest). But the point is this; even great golfers understand that inconsistency is knocking at the door of the one who is not fighting to be consistent.

I believe the Christian experience in some ways compares to this. Life is inconsistent! But steadfast spiritual consistency amid the inconsistencies of life is important for followers. So much so that in James chapter two we have a compelling and interesting case for how to build a more consistent life. Here's what James says as he addresses this topic.

FIRST | THE EVIDENCE OF INCONSISTENCY

First, James invests a lot of time on the effects of playing favorites in the church. His example is vivid. He explains how we treat people inconsistently, how we sometimes favor a rich man over a poor man.

For if a man wearing a gold ring and fine clothing comes into your assembly, and a poor man in shabby clothing also comes in, and if you pay attention to the one who wears the fine clothing and say, "You sit here in a good place," while you say to the poor man, "You stand over there," or, "Sit down at my feet," have you not then made distinctions among yourselves and become judges with evil thoughts?

JAMES 2:2-4

There is not a person alive who has not played favorites. When we play favorites based on several factors, such as race, beliefs, religion, gender, or in this case, our level of income, we do so for the benefits. This is because favoritism sometimes has rewards. We support one friend over another because we anticipate reciprocity. We prefer certain employees over others because they work to advance our agendas. Or we maintain certain relationships over others because they have skills, talents, or gifts that we need from time to time.

One of the most popular expressions of favoritism has a name. It is called *cronyism*, and we witness a lot of this in business and government. *Cronyism* is hiring, honoring, or awarding contracts to people who provide us some financial benefit. Therefore, we give time and attention to these relationships because they have a potential payout. In this chapter James is concerned about *cronyism* in the church and thus the utilization of relationships for personal gain.

James is right to be concerned about this because cronyism and favoritism is an infectious disease. Once it gains momentum it's hard to stop. He even suggests that it can become as abusive and oppressive in the church as it is in the world system.

Are not the rich the ones who oppress you, and the ones who drag you into court? Are they not the ones who blaspheme the honorable name by which you were called?

JAMES 2:6-7

His point is this: the payoff for favoritism is not what you think. The real payoff for favoritism is falsehood and oppression, not financial gain. So James is concerned that falsehood and oppression will find their way into the church's system through *cronyism* and *favoritism*.

James builds on this problem of inconsistency by pointing to the consistent problem of sin.

SECOND | THE CONSISTENT PROBLEM OF SIN

Second, he establishes that when we treat people inconsistently, we display an inconsistent gospel and simultaneously act consistently with the law of sin by playing favorites. This is because sin plays no favorites. We are all guilty of sin.

---

*For whoever keeps the whole law but fails in one point
has become guilty of all of it.*

JAMES 2:10

The point is, we are all guilty of sin. If we have broken one tiny law, we have become guilty of the whole law. This law excludes no one—no race, no heritage, no ability, and no income level (the poor or wealthy). Sin plays no favorites.

And while *"Sin plays no favorites"* may sound bad, it's actually part of what makes the gospel message so good. Regardless of wealth, accomplishment, and gifting, there is no person free from the guilt of sin, which means there is not a person out there who is not in need of God's mercy. This is the truth of God's Law and the basis of the Gospel.

When we play favorites, we act in a manner consistent with the law of sin but witness inconsistently about the good news of Gospel. Remember the poor man and the rich man have equal sin, but in Christ, they also receive equal mercy. To treat them differently communicates an inconsistent message, and James is concerned about this.

---

*So speak and so act as those who are to be judged
under the law of liberty.*

JAMES 2:12

The law of liberty is in direct opposition to any kind of favoritism or cronyism. In fact, the law of liberty nullifies the whole idea of favoritism. This is God's righteous judgment.

So, what do we do to build consistency in our spiritual life? We do this:

THIRD | ERADICATE INCONSISTENCIES WITH CONSISTENT FAITH

I love that James doesn't leave us hanging. He tells us what to do and how to do it. He keeps it simple. We eradicate inconsistencies with a consistent faith.

For the rest of the chapter he spends a great deal of time talking about what faith looks like when it is consistent. Consistent faith is infused with action. It's evidenced by our works. Not the inconsistent works of favoritism, and not the inconsistent works of lip service. But rather a working faith based in the consistent law of liberty.

He is saying our faith must have a connection to good works. The unseen activity of faith is revealed by action; otherwise we become inconsistent.

But to accentuate this point, James makes a shocking connection.

"Even the demons believe—and shudder!"

JAMES 2:19

This is the logical end of belief without works. It's not faith at all. It's a hallow look-alike faith. It appears to be faith but isn't. It's a belief, like that of demons. Now, keep in mind it is a real belief in God, but it's devoid of action that results in fearful convulsions at the sight of God. This is by far the most shocking statement in James's letter, and it makes the point. It's an indictment on belief without action. Belief devoid of action is a demonic look-a-like faith.

Therefore, we are led to the natural conclusion that, to be consistent, our faith must express action. But to counter this memorable and negative example (when he talks about demons), James gives us a positive example, an example that no one would contest; a real example of consistent faith to which all should aspire.

FOURTH | THE FAITH OF FATHER ABRAHAM, WHO WAS A MAN OF CONSISTENT FAITH

No believer would contest Abraham's example. His willingness to walk his son up Mt. Moriah to be sacrificed is perhaps the most incredible story of faith ever told. Abraham, a man, born to a pagan family in a pagan land, heard the voice of God and obeyed:

You see that faith was active along with his works, and faith was completed by his works; and the Scripture was fulfilled that says, "Abraham believed God, and it was counted to him as righteousness"—and he was called a

friend of God. You see that a person is justified by works
and not by faith alone.

JAMES 2:22-24

The overall point is so vivid we can't miss it. Favoritism is an issue of the heart. It's reveals a heart that is inconsistent with a consistent Gospel message. Yet, a man's faith, when coupled with action, indicates the Gospel he believes. Godly action is the evidence of his unseen faith and becomes the witness that the world sees. And this faith is a witness to a consistent God and his law of liberty.

In conclusion, if you were to ask me how to build consistency in your life, then based on what I read here, this is what I would tell you to do:

One, **recall** the consistent law of sin and our need for the law of liberty.

Two, **respond** by being consistent and living out belief in action, which is your working faith.

Third, let this consistency be a witness for God in an unpredictable world of cronyism.

This week take one more step toward being a more consistent follower of God. I would encourage you to pick one place in your spiritual life where you need to be more consistent and spend the next week reflecting and more importantly taking action on that.

REFLECTION & DISCUSSION QUESTIONS

- Where are you inconsistent in your faith?
- How would you like to be more consistent in faith?
- What needs to be done about this, so you can have faith like Abraham?

DEVOTIONALS FOR JAMES 2

PARTIAL FAITH

My brothers, show no partiality as you hold the faith in our Lord Jesus Christ, the Lord of glory. For if a man wearing a gold ring and fine clothing comes into your assembly, and a poor man in shabby clothing also comes in.

JAMES 2:1-2

Like the start of a bad joke, James makes a hard point that isn't hard to miss. *"So two guys walk into a church. One guy is very rich, and the other guy is very poor . . ."* But the punch line is a punch in the face of the presumptuous man who shows partiality! His point is that our eyes see only in part. The human eye never sees the whole picture. But what is seen can result in rapid assumptions and presumptions about the person of another. In this situation, James is concerned that our visual perception might impact our spiritual perception, which leads to drawing the wrong conclusions. This is because in God's family physical status and special treatment will misrepresent the character of God and the community of faith.

The Christian faith looks beyond the physical signs that our world uses to measure status. Our community is driven by a different set of values that sees without partiality because we are aware that we are all sinners, made holy only by God. We must retrain our thoughts in order to fully perceive the view of faith.

ASK THIS: Where do you see partiality in your life?

DO THIS: Pray for an impartial heart that sees with the eyes of an impartial faith.

PRAY THIS: God, may I look beyond what is natural and see the people around me in the way you see them.

THOUGHTS OF EVIL JUDGES

Have you not then made distinctions among yourselves and become judges with evil thoughts?

JAMES 2:4

Some judges do not judge fairly. This is because their thoughts about the world and their motives shape their judgments, which impact their interpretation and decisions on the law. As a result, they make distinctions that favor their preferred future. This is frustrating because it results in an unstable law from judge to judge. What we want is a predictable law and judges who judge predictably.

But in some way, we are all judges. We are people who judge. We make judgments and distinctions among ourselves based on our experiences, likes, and preferences. We make distinctions based on the chemistry we have with others, their character and competency, Often we will have an evil thought as we judge. Right at this moment, we must acknowledge that we, too, will be judged. But as Christians, we know there is only one Law and one Judge. One Law that declares all of us guilty, and One Judge that by his mercy extends grace to a world filled with evil thoughts.

ASK THIS: What evil thoughts do you have in your judgments of others?

DO THIS: Cleanse your thinking, attitude, and action by bringing your judgment to the only fair Judge.

PRAY THIS: God, cleanse me of every evil thought and unjust judgment. May I represent your truth and righteousness by being fair in every judgment I make today.

JUST A SMALL DEVIATION

For whoever keeps the whole law but fails in one point has become guilty of all of it.

JAMES 2:10

Just when you thought perfection was in reach, James writes this. It's a law about the Law: fail once and you're guilty of it all. That's the fatal blow of the law of sin. Sin once and you become a transgressor of the whole thing. But this leads to all kinds of questions. Why do I try so hard to be righteous and avoid failure? Why bother to be righteous when one sin corrupts my whole nature? Why do I still feel guilty after another sinful failure? The answer to each question is Jesus and his sacrifice for the sin of all humanity. His sacrificial death saved, and in Him do we trust.

Therefore, as one trespass led to condemnation for all men, so one act of righteousness leads to justification and life for all men.

ROMANS 5:18

ASK THIS: What unrighteousness is keeping you from God?

DO THIS: Give your sin to God and ask him for salvation.

PRAY THIS: God, I need you today. I acknowledge that my life is corrupted by sin. I bring my unrighteousness to you and receive your righteousness. Be the Lord and leader of my life today and every day.

WHICH DO YOU WANT? MERCY OR JUSTICE?

For judgment is without mercy to one who has shown no mercy. Mercy triumphs over judgment.

JAMES 2:13

Strict judgment is what we want for other people, but not for ourselves. What we want for ourselves is mercy. So why the duality? Usually this is because we have innocently suffered the sin. Therefore, we think, *"They deserve strict judgment."* But remember, we are not free from accusation. We, too, are sinners. We, too, have caused unfair suffering. And we deserve justice. So don't opt for strict justice when you want mercy. Instead, show mercy and break the cycle, so that the final judgment you receive is not without mercy.

ASK THIS: To whom do you need to show mercy?

DO THIS: Show mercy.

PRAY THIS: God, may I learn to be merciful in an unmerciful world. And through this may I know your mercy and with it the freedom of merciful judgment.

WORKING FAITH

*What good is it, my brothers, if someone says he has faith
but does not have works?*

JAMES 2:14

While we may not see the inclination of a person's faith, we can definitely see its impact. While works never earn a person's salvation, our faith should display works. Faith should have a noticeable impact on the people around us. It should make visible what is invisible, by our word and deed. So, if you have faith, work it out! Don't be a person of faith who lacks work. What good is that?

ASK THIS: What step of faith do you need to take today?

DO THIS: What action will result from this step?

PRAY THIS: God, may my faith be visible. May my work be the evidence of my faith. And may I only do this work for your glory. In Christ's name, Amen.

DON'T IGNORE THE NEED

If a brother or sister is poorly clothed and lacking in daily food, and one of you says to them, "Go in peace, be warmed and filled," without giving them the things needed for the body, what good is that?

JAMES 2:15-16

I hate to admit it, but I have done this. I have ignored people in need. I do it most when I am most consumed with myself. I rationalize my time, concerns, and needs, and therefore I elevate them above others' needs. But let's not ignore the divine importance of each and every moment. We are spiritual beings having a physical experience. Therefore, as we are presented with a physical need, we should not be dismissive, but respond with a spiritual urgency. Why should we act? Because this is what faith looks like. Faith recognizes that God has placed a person (with a specific need) before us because he knew only we could fulfill it.

ASK THIS: Who is a brother or sister in Christ with a physical need?

DO THIS: Today, as you see a need—fulfill it—and you will discover how meeting a physical need changes the spiritual trajectory in others and yourself.

PRAY THIS: God, show me a need. May I act immediately. May I have the resource to fulfill it.

EVEN DEMONS BELIEVE

You believe that God is one; you do well. Even the demons believe—and shudder!

JAMES 2:19

This is a shocking verse. A shocking truth that our belief may be no different than that of a demon? We see that demons, spiritual beings opposed to God, still actively believe. But hopefully our belief is different—we believe that God is real and so act on this belief. For belief without action is no different from that of demons. Don't shudder or convulse in fear at the coming of God. Demonstrate an active faith! Don't put on a show but live out a faith that is different than demons.

ASK THIS: Is your faith merely belief without action?

DO THIS: Activate your unseen faith and fuse it with action.

PRAY THIS: God, I believe. Show me today one thing I need to do. Make my faith and its action a witness for the world.

FROM FOOLISH TO WISE TALK

OPENING QUESTIONS

- Why do we say foolish things?
- When it comes to speech, in what environment do you blow it the most?
- How would you like to improve?

CHAPTER 3

I cannot tell you how many times I have said something I've regretted. Seriously, there have been numerous (if not hundreds) of times in my life that I said something I wished would've stayed in my head and not come out my mouth. Just ask my wife if you need a witness to my verbal stupidity.

But eventually, every man puts his foot in his mouth. This happens a lot in moments when we

- *Fail to filter out sensitive information.*
- *Fail to get control of our emotions before we speak.*
- *Fail to realize that what we say might be offensive.*
- *Fail to get more information before offering an opinion.*

But there is something even more tragic about the impact of our words than just the embarrassment of putting our foot in our mouth. Mainly, it's how our words impact another person spiritually and thus impair that person's ability to see, hear, and know the message of Christ. This is what James addresses.

In chapter three, we will dig into this issue and discover the power we have with the words we speak. James will show us that what we say impacts people and exposes our character. Even more, it affects our identity. What we say makes us either foolish or wise.

FIRST | OUR FOOLISHNESS

The first thing James does in this chapter is address the foolish things we say that make us look foolish. He lays blame to a single muscle of the body: *the tongue.* It's a small but powerful muscle of the mouth used for tasting, licking, and swallowing. Yet in humans the tongue has a unique power that goes beyond this. It's the primary muscle used for articulating speech and therefore is a necessary tool for communicating, teaching, directing, and guiding.

Therefore, with the tongues that we are given, we possess great power, a power similar to that of a rudder on a great ship driven by a powerful wind. Here is how James describes it:

Look at the ships also: though they are so large and are driven by strong winds, they are guided by a very small rudder wherever the will of the pilot directs. So also the tongue is a small member, yet it boasts of great things.

JAMES 3:4-5

This is not some new idea. We've all known this based on the power we've experiences from an influential teacher, coach, politician, or athlete. The tongue possesses immense power to guide a great many people in a direction toward God or away from him. Thus toward foolishness or wisdom.

But here's a question for you: *Is the tongue really to blame?*

The answer, of course, is "yes" and "no." It's the person who uses the tongue that bears ultimate blame. And even more accurately, the tongue is simply a tool that does the bidding of the desires, thoughts, and words that come from our mouth. As a result, the tongue can be used for great good or great evil.

James makes this same claim.

From the same mouth come blessing and cursing.

JAMES 3:10

We have all experienced this. There is not a person alive who has not been eviscerated by the words of another human being. This never feels good, even when it may be justified. At the same time we have all been moved by the kind and encouraging words of someone we love, by a simple loving, soft-spoken, and kind word.

But James takes this a bit further. He emphasizes the point and the impact by recognizing the potential downside to the tongue's inappropriate use. It's that the tongue can be weaponized. James alluded to this at the beginning of the chapter. Here is what he said in verse 1

Not many of you should become teachers, my brothers, for you know that we who teach will be judged with greater strictness.

JAMES 3:1

His point is that the teacher's role carries with it a special responsibility, and thus a stricter judgment. (But again, this is nothing new.)

People who teach can shape the future, and sometimes they shape it intentionally in their direction. Some manipulate the truth ever so carefully to favor their ideas, opinions, worldviews, and perspectives. They possess the power to influence the minds of unsuspecting people. Some very charismatic voices have led people down deadly paths. Take 20th-century examples like Adolf Hitler, Kim Jong-Un, Joseph Stalin, or Saddam Hussein. Each of these men has used their voice to influence millions and guide unsuspecting people toward devastation. Like these examples, all leaders will be judged for how they have influenced people. And as James says, their judgment will be stricter.

Yet people like you and I possess the same power. Just because we don't lead millions of people doesn't mean we don't have the same ability. By God's design we are given a tongue to influence others. We are all called to teach, and even exercise power with our tongues. If you recall, God gave mankind creative power to define and name things at the beginning of time:

The man gave names to all livestock and to the birds of the heavens and to every beast of the field.

GENESIS 2:20

God gave us our tongues and allowed us the freedom to use them to create and define things within his divine order. This is a unique and impressive power that we must steward with care. We are commanded to use this power and responsibility in a godly way. Now, more than ever in our country and world, we need God-honoring voices to stand up and use their tongues to good rather than do evil. In the roles we are given we need to be a counterforce for good in this world that speaks nothing but foolishness.

James sets us up to discover how to speak what is right and righteous by pursuing God's Wisdom.

SECOND | GOD'S WISDOM

In this chapter, James presents the real issue with the tongue: it's the heart itself. You see, the problem is not only what our tongues say. It's not merely how the muscle of the tongue articulates a variety of words we put together into sentences. But more, it's a problem of the human heart.

Who is wise and understanding among you?
By his good conduct, let him show his works in the
meekness of wisdom. But if you have bitter jealousy
and selfish ambition in your hearts, do not boast
and be false to the truth.

JAMES 3:13-14

Here we finally get to the core issue: it's a heart-driven by *jealousy* and *selfishness*. You see, we have devious hearts that can be passionately selfish. Thus our emotions direct us to say and do some unfortunate and foolish things. But the secret in this verse lies in what *guides* our tongue. Do we let feelings determine the movement of our tongue? Or do we let the truth determine the movement of our tongue? If it's our emotions, then our tongues become unstable and selfish. If it's the truth of God, then we are understanding, stable, and wise Christians who conduct ourselves rightly.

Here is the gamechanger. James takes this one step further. He shows us how to *gain* wisdom. It's incredible. It's found in the single greatest verse in this chapter.

But the wisdom from above is first pure, then peaceable, gentle, open to reason, full of mercy and good fruits, impartial and sincere.

JAMES 3:17

This is a remarkable insight. It's full of wisdom for the man of God. James is aware that true wisdom only comes from above.

The wise person does these six things:

- *Is open to conversation and reason.*
- *Handles situations peacefully.*
- *Judges impartially.*
- *Uses power mercifully.*
- *Exhibits good fruit.*
- *Does it all from a pure and sincere heart.*

This describes the wise. This is what they do.

So, what concrete actions can we take in response to these verses?

There are at least two. First, if you find yourself using your tongue in foolish ways, you can begin by stopping those behaviors. Start by choosing not to make those statements or use those phrases and words you're in the habit of saying. You know the words, phrases, or statements that you make which hurt other people. Just choose to stop saying those things. Go all-in and remove these words and phrases from your language. For example, if cursing is a problem—stop cursing. If sarcasm is a problem—stop saying sarcastic things. If an emotion like anger is a problem—stop opening your mouth when you are angry.

Second, there's also a proactive step we can take to increase the wisdom that comes from our mouth. You see, it's not always enough to merely stop negative behaviors. It's good also to have that positive counter-response, to start positive and godly ones. I think James has a pretty good checklist for becoming wiser people who say wiser things. His list of 6 things is strong:

- *Be open to conversation and reason.*
- *Handle situations peacefully.*
- *Be impartial in judgments.*
- *Uses power mercifully.*
- *Exhibit good fruit.*
- *Do it all from a pure and sincere heart.*

You could easily choose one thing from this list and replace that one bad behavior with a good one. One that will guide you toward wisdom and using your tongue with wisdom.

But don't miss this: we are not merely list-switching here, switching from a list of bad behaviors to a list of good ones. No. We are using our tongue, and thus our behaviors, to reign in our hearts that need to come under the Lordship of Jesus Christ. Let's go back to the very beginning of this chapter. In verse three, James says this.

If we put bits into the mouths of horses so that they obey us, we guide their whole bodies as well.

JAMES 3:3

That's what we are trying to do. We are putting a bit in our mouth, or on our tongue, not merely to reign in our tongue or our behaviors, but our hearts. Remember, this is all connect to our heart. We are turning our desires, and thus our whole lives by bridling this tiny little muscle.

So now let's get out there and do something with this message. Act on it!

REFLECTION & DISCUSSION QUESTIONS

- Does this lesson regarding the use of your tongue convict you in any area?
- Which one of these six things can you choose to improve upon?
  - ☐ *Be open to conversation and reason.*
  - ☐ *Handle situations peacefully.*
  - ☐ *Be impartial in judgments.*
  - ☐ *Uses power mercifully.*
  - ☐ *Exhibit good fruit.*
  - ☐ *Do it all from a pure and sincere heart.*

DEVOTIONALS FOR JAMES 3

STRICT JUDGMENT

> *Not many of you should become teachers, my brothers,*
> *for you know that we who teach will be judged with*
> *greater strictness.*

JAMES 3:1

Every time I read these words; I pause.

As a teacher of God's Word for many years, I have discovered the weight behind this statement. No doubt James understood this as well. He was one of the first teachers in the first church ever established, the church of Jerusalem. His letter was a traveling teaching that carried a message that reached many churches in the Mediterranean.

So if you aspire to teach God's Word, never forget the *"greater strictness."* These words are not the words of men, but God. This Bible was written down by fallible men who bore the Gospel's weight. It's God's inspired words, not man's, and we should treat them as such.

ASK THIS: Do you treat every word you read in the Bible with care, acting on it as the very Word of God?

DO THIS: Revere God's Word and the God of the Bible.

PRAY THIS: God, I love you. Thanks for speaking to me through the Bible, which is the very word that came from you.

SET ABLAZE

*So also the tongue is a small member,
yet it boasts of great things. How great a forest
is set ablaze by such a small fire!*

JAMES 3:5

A small spark can cause great damage. Many of us know first-hand the power of small fires. The same is true of our tongue. That small muscle within our mouth lights fires all the time. Fires that have ramifications in people's lives that last a lifetime. Phrases like "you always" and "you never" start great fires. Shouts like "I hate you," brand fiery scars onto the human heart. Quick-tempered declarations like "I'm not sure I ever loved you," sear the soul. But even though we have felt the fire of words like these, we often don't consider the effects when we say these things ourselves. Too late we realize that we cannot retract these sparks of words that have started a fire we cannot stop.

ASK THIS: What words did you say yesterday that have started a fire today?

DO THIS: Give attention to the words you spoke yesterday and the ones you will speak today.

PRAY THIS: God, shut my mouth when I am about to say something that will hurt the Gospel's spread in a person's life. I know your words give life, so let not mine get in your way.

UNTAMED

For every kind of beast and bird, of reptile and sea creature, can be tamed and has been tamed by mankind, but no human being can tame the tongue. It is a restless evil, full of deadly poison.

JAMES 3:7-8

I'm sorry, but I laugh every time I read these words from James. The hyperbole is extreme and yet simultaneously spot on. Can we really tame wild animals but not the tongue? And yet, all we need to do is to do to tame the tongue is close our lips! Then, to add insult to injury, James says it's "full of deadly poison." So right when I want to laugh I consider all the restless evil and venomous poison I have spewed on the world. And then immediately, all the injurious memories of hurtful words spewed by others come flooding back—and my laughter turns to mourning.

ASK THIS: How do you need to tame your untamed tongue?

DO THIS: Close your upper and lower lips together before saying something you'll regret.

PRAY THIS: God, forgive me for my venomous words.

THE MEEKNESS OF WISDOM

Who is wise and understanding among you?
By his good conduct, let him show his works in the
meekness of wisdom.

JAMES 3:13

To be meek is not to be weak. Meekness requires stamina, long-suffering, patience, and self-will. Too often we fail to see the nature of this word and confuse it with cowardice. But this is an unwise comparison. The older we get, the more we realize that meekness means bringing conduct into submission, and with this comes a pearl of great wisdom. So are you ready to conduct good works in the wisdom of meekness?

ASK THIS: What one action do you need to take today to be meek and thus wise?

DO THIS: Take that action.

PRAY THIS: God, give me the courage to be meek. Help me stand fast when afflicted, to be strong when I feel weak. And God, make me wiser.

VILE PRACTICES

For where jealousy and selfish ambition exist, there will be disorder and every vile practice.

JAMES 3:16

Do you ever wonder why there is so much disorder in the world today? What is the root cause of all our issues: rioting, disease, violence, addiction, terrorism, racism, and political controversies? These issues arise not because we are inherently moral and righteous people but because of our jealousy and selfish ambitions. Jealousy arises from thoughts or feelings of insecurity and fear in response to present deficiencies. But when these jealousies combine with a selfish ambition, they are a one-two punch resulting in disorder, producing vile practices.

ASK THIS: What jealousy and selfish ambition do you need to address?

DO THIS: Find your provision and value in God.

PRAY THIS: God, help me stop contributing to our world's disorder and vile practices today. Change my heart and make me more like you.

WISDOM'S PROCESS

But the wisdom from above is first pure, then peaceable, gentle, open to reason, full of mercy and good fruits, impartial and sincere.

JAMES 3:17

This is a remarkable insight. It's full of wisdom for any follower of God. James is aware that true wisdom only comes from above. The wise followers does six things:

- *Handles every situation in a manner that is peaceful and gentle.*
- *Open to conversation yet knows godly reason only comes from above.*
- *Merciful, knowing that harm could be inflicted with his authority and power.*
- *Fruitful in righteousness and good deeds.*
- *Makes impartial judgments.*
- *Motivated from a pure and sincere heart.*

There's your checklist for today. Work on one aspect and grow in wisdom's process.

ASK THIS: What characteristic of wisdom do you need to work on?

DO THIS: Work it and be wiser today than yesterday.

PRAY THIS: God, give me supernatural wisdom from above. Make me as wise as Solomon.

JAMES

NEW DESIRES RESULT IN NEW ACTIONS

OPENING QUESTIONS

- What wrong desires are most common in our world today?
- What wrong actions result from these wrong desires?
- Is it possible to change a person's desires?
- How do we do this?

CHAPTER 4

I have met many followers who want something different from this life than their current experience. Yet many never change. There are several reasons they don't achieve the change they want. First, some don't change because life, as is, is simply good enough. Second, others want to change but often are stumped in knowing what step to take next. Third, others may want to change but lack the passion or the courage to make it happen. And finally, there are those who try. They give a full effort, but then fail a few times to make the change and then give up altogether.

We must remember that change is possible. If either the pain or the incentives are high enough, most will change. We will adjust our diet, activities, behaviors, and relationships when the pain or incentives are high enough, which tells me change is possible. But this approach is a reactive approach to change. Is there a positive and more proactive approach change?

I think there are plenty of Christians out there who want a better life and change. People who want to be spiritually proactive rather than reactive. In this chapter, James will show us how to pursue this with two essential actions.

ESSENTIAL ACTION ONE | PURSUE NEW DESIRES

If you want lasting change in life, you have to go beyond behavior modification. I know many people that spend time switching from a list of bad behaviors to a list of good behaviors in the spiritual life. While this can produce results, they are usually minimal and, in the end, it does not produce lasting change.

For example, how many times have you heard someone say I'm going to quit smoking, cursing, lying, or drinking? Or, on the other hand, how many times have you heard someone say I am going to start dieting, working out, or building spiritual discipline on a more regular basis? (By the way, these are all great behaviors to stop and start.) They are worthy goals. But sometimes the change we want just doesn't happen because we are focusing our energy and effort on the wrong thing.

The only way to pursue lasting change is to permanently redirect the desires themselves, and let the behaviors follow. We have to want not only a behavior to change but we must also change the desires themselves. This is a change of a person at the deepest level. This is why Jesus calls his followers to such a radical commitment. He wants commitment to him to take precedence over all other commitments and desires. Jesus knows our desires determine our direction. In this chapter, James helps us to see how to do this. It's a two-fold action. Listen to this verse. It's one of the best in this chapter.

Submit yourselves therefore to God. Resist the devil, and he will flee from you.

JAMES 4:7

Do you see the action and counteraction? Do you see his one-two punch for pursuing a deeper change of the desires? It's a deadly boxing combo—a jab of *submission* with an uppercut of *resistance*. You see, James makes clear that resisting temptation is not enough. Resistance by human effort misses the spiritual emphasis. Resistance without the Holy Spirit is simply list switching or behaviors switching. And it's exhausting. We may try it, but at some point, we will switch back without effective spiritual help.

James is clear in this text; sin is fought with a supernatural effort of submission. James implies we no longer submit to the desires of the enemy, which gives him his power. Instead, we submit to God and let his power resist the spiritual force of evil that opposes us. This is not merely a human effort. It's a supernatural one-two combo that makes the Devil flee. In submission to God, the desires for him resist that of the Devil.

Submission is resistance. Submission leads to the change we want because this affects the desires in a man.

And if you are wondering what this looks like, James is going to tell us.

ESSENTIAL TWO | BRING OUR DESIRES UNDER THE WILL OF GOD

Later in this chapter James digs into what this looks like practically. And he is pretty straightforward about it.

> *Come now, you who say, "Today or tomorrow we will go into such and such a town and spend a year there and trade and make a profit"— yet you do not know what tomorrow will bring. What is your life? For you are a mist that appears for a little time and then vanishes.*
>
> **JAMES 4:13-14**

I love this section. It may feel a little cryptic, but James tells us that our short-term desires (and thus our short-term plans) don't always align with God's long-term strategy. We have all encountered moments like this. These moments are humbling. Frequently we learn that our desires were miss-aligned because there was something we wanted, while God wanted something different. When this happens (which it will) we are sometimes disappointed to discover that God's will and ours did not line up like we thought because we got so carried away by a potential profit or personal benefit. And because this thing we want potentially profits us, and we ended up losing sight of God and his will.

But James shows us how to get aligned. It's remarkably simple.

Instead you ought to say, "If the Lord wills, we will live and do this or that." As it is, you boast in your arrogance. All such boasting is evil. So whoever knows the right thing to do and fails to do it, for him it is sin.

JAMES 4:15-17

Here is how we bring our desires under the submission of God's will. We preach to our desires frequently—*frequently*—just as James suggests we do here. You may note we don't have a problem preaching to others when we are boasting! That's his point. When we are proud of ourselves, we don't have a problem singing our praises or boasting about our desires. This boasting is just reinforcement for the flesh. Should we not do the same thing for those of us who live by the Spirit? Should we not proclaim God's will to our desires and give God credit when he does something great through us?

I think the phrase, *"God's will, not mine"* could be four transformation words to preach regularly to all your desires. These four words could be the transformational preaching your behaviors need. And it might transform more than just one behavior—it could change all of them.

This is the point. Behaviors follow the desires; so start desiring Him and your behaviors will change. We give up our will for his will in everything we do and ask God to provide us direction, as James instructed us earlier in the chapter. Then we resist the desire to boast, and we do what is right and righteous. We repeat this again and again.

So here's my challenge for you this week. I want you to say this phrase each day to yourself this week.

God's will, not mine.

Say it three times a day: morning, noon, and night. Preach to your desires consistently and see if it doesn't result in something good and beautiful in your life.

REFLECTION & DISCUSSION QUESTIONS

- Where in your life do you need to pursue new desires?
- How can you bring present wrongful desires under the will of God?
- How would you like to ask for help from God?

DEVOTIONALS FOR JAMES 4

THE WAR'S WITHIN

What causes quarrels and what causes fights among you? Is it not this that your passions are at war within you?

JAMES 4:1

Quarrels and fights are external expressions of something that happens *within* a person. The root issue is the uncontrolled passion within us. It's the war we fight within ourselves with our desires. We desire to do good but there is another desire as well—a desire to do bad. This is born from a vengeful spirit resulting from sin and injustice that becomes violent toward others. The cycle repeats unless by the Spirit we call an end to the war within and thus end the war without.

ASK THIS: What war are you fighting within?

DO THIS: Make peace with God and end the war.

PRAY THIS: God, bring peace to my spirit so that I will not wound the spirit of others.

HAVE YOU ASKED?

You covet and cannot obtain, so you fight and quarrel.
You do not have, because you do not ask. You ask and do
not receive, because you ask wrongly,
to spend it on your passions.

JAMES 4:2-3

If you thought James was challenging yesterday, well, he gets even more challenging today. But honestly, he's right. Most of the time, we do not have because we do not ask—that's just the truth. I cannot tell you how many times I thought about something, complained about something, or talked about something—yet failed to ask for something! But when I do ask, I find that God and others are willing to give.

So today, when you are prompted with any need, how about just asking God?

- *Do you want a closer relationship with your wife, kids, and God? Ask him!*
- *Do you need income and provision? Ask him!*
- *Do you need saving from a repetitive sin? Ask him!*
- *Do you need hope in despair? Ask him!*
- *Do you need meaningful relationships in loneliness? Ask him!*

ASK THIS: What is it you need?

DO THIS: Ask him.

PRAY THIS: God, please meet my need for _____.

NOT OPPOSED

But he gives more grace. Therefore it says, "God opposes the proud but gives grace to the humble."

JAMES 4:6

I think some think God is opposed to them. But this is a misunderstanding. The God of the Bible has been in active pursuit of fallen people since our very first sin. It is mankind who has been in opposition to God. It's pride that stands in the way. Yet our arrogant opposition does not stop God. His eternal grace reaches farther than our temporal disobedience. So resist opposition and pride and enjoy union with God. Be humble and discover a God who gives more grace.

ASK THIS: What form of pride do you need to lay down?

DO THIS: Replace pride with humility.

PRAY THIS: God, receive the offering of my pride, and shower me with your grace. I need it today!

THE RESISTANCE

Submit yourselves therefore to God.
Resist the Devil, and he will flee from you.

JAMES 4:7

This is the one-two punch. It's a jab of submission with an uppercut of resistance. Remember resistance is not enough, but submission with resistance is, because it's a full effort. So don't just stop a negative behavior, start a positive one. Submit all of who you are to God and then resist and watch how rapidly the Devil flees. In this way it is not just your behavioral resistance but a supernatural and spiritual effort backed by God. In this way God's counterforce becomes a spiritual force through you.

ASK THIS: What issue do you need to submit to God today?

DO THIS: Submit the issue and resist the Devil.

PRAY THIS: God, I need a supernatural effort today. I submit my desires, thoughts, and actions to you. Give me supernatural strength to resist the Devil; in Jesus's name may he flee.

A RESPONSIVE GOD

Draw near to God, and he will draw near to you.

JAMES 4:8

There are moments in life that we conclude that God isn't working. These moments almost exclusively happen when we experience a setback, tragedy, or injustice that we believe is undeserved. And here's the deal: in these moments we want God to respond to us most! Sometimes, we fail to hear the response we so desperately expect, and we conclude God's not there. But we forget God has been drawing near to man since the beginning of time. He is working out a great divine plan, and sometimes this plan eludes us. Our response should be to keep drawing near. Draw near despite the enemy's illusion that God isn't doing his part, for the truth is there is nothing that's going to stop God from loving his finest creation—that's you!

ASK THIS: Does God feel far?

DO THIS: Don't believe the illusion; keep drawing near.

PRAY THIS: God, I need you. Today I come only because I need you. Guide me. Help me. Save me.

THE UP DOWN LIFE

---

*Be wretched and mourn and weep. Let your laughter
be turned to mourning and your joy to gloom. Humble
yourselves before the Lord, and he will exalt you.*

JAMES 4:9-10

James has been trying to sear this thought into our thick heads: that there is a way about our desires and actions, that leads to mourning, weeping, and gloom. It all begins with something wretched within each of us. A simple desire that has miserable outcomes. This brings us all down.

But there is another way, one that brings the desires before the Lord. It requires us to do something that calls for the greatest of strength—humbling ourselves. But here's the best part: the humble is the one who is laughing, joyful, and exalted. It's a little counterintuitive, but the outcomes are better. And the action is simple—go low before God and let him lift you up.

ASK THIS: Do you feel down?

DO THIS: Go humble, and let God bring you up.

PRAY THIS: God, accept my humility and fragility as a sacrifice today. I come low and ask you to lift me.

GOD'S PLANTS VS. OUR PLANS

Come now, you who say, "Today or tomorrow we will go into such and such a town and spend a year there and trade and make a profit"— yet you do not know what tomorrow will bring. What is your life? For you are a mist that appears for a little time and then vanishes.

JAMES 4:13-14

Some of us are planners and others of us are not. This admonition of James is not merely about planning. It has more to do with how our plans compete with God's plans. It addresses the intentional exclusion of God from our plans.

Most won't admit that we exclude God, but there is something about a person when they get a dream, idea, or vision in their head. They tend to move toward self-interest rather than God's interests. This results in thinking that forgets one thing—the brevity of life. That this life is but a mist. That this life and all our grandiose plans will soon vanish.

This is our reminder today: make plans—but don't forget to plan for the one thing that really matters. Eternity! Eternity is a very long time, and tomorrow is not, for it will soon become yesterday.

ASK THIS: Do you tend to leave God out of your plans?

DO THIS: Make a decision today that has an eternal impact— learn today to make plans daily for eternity.

PRAY THIS: God, today I lay my plans down for your plans. I pray you will accomplish your will in my life. Help me focus on eternity, and not just today and tomorrow.

DO THE RIGHT THING

So whoever knows the right thing to do
and fails to do it, for him it is sin.

JAMES 4:17

This is one of the great axioms of James. His concern is that Christians sometimes choose to lose consciousness when it comes to doing the right thing. In other words, we make proud proclamations about our Christian title, our belief in the birth and resurrection of Jesus, and that the Bible is our rule for right living. But then we do things that act in contradiction with these claims, beliefs, and rules. These actions are our sins. These actions reveal our willful loss of consciousness.

But . . .

This makes the axiom simple. Just do the right thing—all the time—and then you'll not need to worry about the axiom.

ASK THIS: Is there any inconsistency you know of, that you need to address this year?

DO THIS: Bring that issue to God and leave it with him.

PRAY THIS: God, help my knowing and doing to be fused together.

THREE ACTIONS OF GREAT FOLLOWERS

OPENING QUESTIONS

- Mankind was created for action. Why?
- When we act wrongly and unbiblically what results? Why?
- How could one godly action from one person, change everything? Can you give an example?

CHAPTER 5

Edmund Burke once said: *"The only thing necessary for the triumph of evil is for good men to do nothing."*

This is a profound thought. Burke emphasizes two things. First, that evil will triumph if we are apathetic. Second, that good men are called to take action against the progressive nature of evil. It's a call on those who are *"good,"* or I might take a little liberty here and correct Burke and suggest it's a call upon the *"righteous"* to no longer be silent or apathetic toward evil.

You know, the problems we have today are not new; they are just more exposed today than ever before. This season of our life is exposing our need for righteousness in a world of evil and sinful people. I think most of us don't like what we see. We may not even like who we are becoming. And we can do something. I believe within each of us; as Christians, we want to do great things. We feel positioned to act. We feel called to act. But to act rightly we must get some simple things right.

That's what I have loved about every chapter of the letter of James. James keeps things simple. He hits the simple things hard. Like a coach prepping his team, he pounds on some repetitive practices. This final chapter, chapter five, is no different. James addresses some relatively simple spiritual practices that move us to take the right action. He speaks of three actions of great followers.

ACTION ONE | AN EYE FOR TRUE PROSPERITY

First, the righteous have an eye for true prosperity.

James begins this chapter with one of the strongest condemnations you'll read anywhere in the Bible to the wealthy and rich. He insists that the pursuit of wealth results in oppression and fraud and will eventually make for a miserable end for those who pursue it.

But in verse five, He gets after the core issue.

> *You have lived on the earth in luxury and in self-indulgence. You have fattened your hearts in a day of slaughter.*
>
> **JAMES 5:5**

His point is fantastic. It's that we can invest the time we have here indulging luxury. Many pursue this path. They intentionally get *"fat"* seeking the luxuries of this life. But James warns that those who do this are only preparing themselves for a gory end. This is because to do so is very short-sighted. It's foolish because it misses the sight of an eternity full of riches. This is the tension of being a Christian in a materialistic world.

James has been preaching this warning since chapter one. There is a joy found in suffering that is greater than the pursuit of personal happiness. When we connect the joy of suffering in chapter one to the point he makes in chapter five, we discover why. Suffering in this life is nothing compared to the luxuries of eternity. Therefore, we can conclude we have two choices on how to live. We can be rich here, or rich there. We can have riches temporarily, or be rich permanently. The wise man would be right to choose the latter and forgo temporary happiness to have eternal joy, riches, luxury, and lasting prosperity.

Yet the allure of temporary happiness and momentary prosperity has conned many. I think this is James's warning to us, that there are dangers in riches. They make us *fat*—not in just weight put on by excessive calories. He means that we get fat on selfishness. This selfishness will result in physical gluttony, but spiritual starvation. These selfish desires are always lurking. The temptation is right around the corner, and therefore we need to be alert, alert to the pull of temporary prosperity.

I know many preach against a prosperity gospel—one that promises great riches in our time. But in this situation, I must say there is prosperity—one of spiritual proportions. In this sense, we aim for a better prosperity, one of great blessing, where we will be fat in the promises of Christ in an eternity with Him. And God promises this. Now *that's* a prosperity gospel.

ACTION TWO | LIVE PATIENTLY

Second, great followers live patiently. In the second part of this chapter, James guides us to understand a character trait important to all followers—patience. The endurance to suffer longer in light of the Lord's eventual return.

"Be patient, therefore, brothers, until the coming of the Lord. See how the farmer waits for the precious fruit of the earth, being patient about it, until it receives the early and the late rains."

JAMES 5:7

I love the addition of the short illustration in his call for patience. It illuminates something significant. It's something that we all need to hear. It's that there are many things out of our control. In those moments life is coming undone, we do not need more control, but more patience.

Every farmer understands this. There are some elements of farming that are entirely in the hands of God, like the weather and natural resources. In season, all farmers experience some level of anxiety about natural provisions that they cannot control—specifically the weather. In this way, James tells us what we all need to hear about the challenges we each face. There are things that are out of our control and thus drive us to dependence on God. In these situations, we need patience— not control.

In our time I think many want to control the unfolding situations in our world. We feel uncertain. In our uncertainty or anxiety, we look for ways to control what's happening. We do this because we want some certainty. But this storm is not going to be weathered with human control. We must turn to God and nurture patience. Patience does not mean we should sit around and do nothing. If God calls us to speak and act on his behalf we should do that. But until that moment comes, we cannot ignore that we need to act patiently, trusting a God who is in control.

God is patient and we should be too. We should exude this attribute because we know that there are elements of life we cannot control. We should be wise enough to realize we could try something in our own effort, but it would be a waste of time, and therefore we choose patience. Listen again as James drives the point home:

"Behold, we consider those blessed who remained steadfast. You have heard of the steadfastness of Job, and you have seen the purpose of the Lord, how the Lord is compassionate and merciful."

JAMES 5:11

I love that he uses one of the best illustrations of patience and steadfastness in the Bible—Job. Job is one of the earliest books of the Bible, and his life is an illustration of patience. By the end of Job chapter one, we discover that he has lost everything. Children—gone. Cattle—gone. Fields—gone. Health—gone. The only thing left is him and his wife and a few so-called friends.

But in the middle of Job's suffering, we see that he never gives up. We read chapters of dialogue and debate. Even many a moment when Job could have just quit on God altogether. But he doesn't; he suffers longer—he builds patience. Right when you think he is about to give up and he starts questioning God. Then God steps in and questions him. God confronts him as a God who is in control. In the end we watch as God blesses him again, not just with temporal riches, but with a face-to-face encounter with God himself.

James makes a great point. The purposes of God are accomplished in the patient. The one who exudes patience, and therefore suffers longer, enjoys the pleasure of seeing the purposes of God. Do you see that? This one gets to see God through good times and bad. And thus, as James states, only the patient witnesses the compassion and mercies of God. The question is, is this you?

ACTION THREE | CONFESS PRAYERFULLY

Third, great followers confess prayerfully.

In this final chapter, James's conclusion is strong.

"Therefore, confess your sins to one another and pray for one another, that you may be healed. The prayer of a righteous person has great power as it is working."

JAMES 5:16

I think many Christians, have a hard time opening up about their challenges and shortcomings. And there are many reasons we hide. Yet when the pressure gets to be too much we will eventually be pressured into the discomfort and comfort of opening up. And in this last chapter James reminds us to confess, which should be more common practice in the church.

Confession is a word that means *"to agree with God."* And really to agree with him about what he already knows. It's to tell God the truth about yourself. You see, we think we can hide from God. But it's not possible. James wants us to confess to God. But he adds a little nuance—he also wants us to *confess our sins to one another*. To open up about the issues we are facing—and I think this is hard for so many. Yet there is great power in doing this because confession joined with prayer results in righteous prayer with great power.

There is remarkable freedom in living consciously free before God. Followers that do share rather openly about who they are and what they have done. The one who does business in confession is a great follower. Practicing this in the company of trusting people is valuable. And then, even better, we then pray together, and then God heals.

So here is James's final charge in chapter five to us. He says great Christians take spiritual action in these ways

- *They have an eye for true prosperity.*
- *They live patiently.*
- *They confess prayerfully.*

And with this comes great power.

We have taken a journey through time with James, the brother of Jesus: a man that was no stranger to challenges. He has challenged us. I bet if he we alive today and could shout one word of encouragement to us as he would shout this word.

Stand fast!

Stand fast as a follower of God. So today be encouraged by his words. A man who played with Jesus as a child and a man who saw the resurrected Lord shouts to you "*Stand fast*" in that trial you are facing, as eternity is just around the corner and a time of great celebration is coming.

REFLECTION & DISCUSSION QUESTIONS

- In which of the three actions do you need to improve?
- What one thing can you do to improve in that one action?
- How could another person help or support you in becoming great?

DEVOTIONALS FOR JAMES 5

AWAITING THE RICH

Come now, you rich, weep and howl
for the miseries that are coming upon you.

JAMES 5:1

This chapter begins with one sharp condemnation. It feels like a talk-down to a disobedient son who has just wronged his father.

But let's agree: we've all dreamed of the vanities of wealth. Some of us have intentionally pursued this path, either successfully and unsuccessfully. After reading this our dreams of vanity might be better off unrealized, for it appears that the rich will soon experience a nightmare that results in weeping and howling. So don't let your vain pursuit of dreams of wealth pursue you.

ASK THIS: What are you pursuing?

DO THIS: Make your pursuit holy, and pursue God with all you have, even your money.

PRAY THIS: God, purify my heart and my every pursuit this year.

A STAMPEDE OF JUDGMENT

You have condemned and murdered the righteous person. He does not resist you.

JAMES 5:6

Truly righteous followers are patient in suffering. Case in point: Jesus Christ.

I have to admit there are moments when I experience acts of condemnation by others that something wells up in me. This thing within me is not good and not righteous. Therefore I am ready with a defensive response—ready to rise up. Yet James, in his day, watched as his people experienced oppression, and even murder, by the hands of oppressors. Many of the oppressed did not resist these evil acts. They were like *"a lamb that is led to the slaughter."*

So today, you may encounter an oppressor. It could be right for you to speak out and stand up and do this righteously. But there is a second possibility, that God may want you to resist not the wrongdoer. But either way, know this—God's judgment is coming! It's coming like a stampede that will not be stopped and his righteousness will win out over every act of unrighteousness you have endured.

He was oppressed and he was afflicted, yet he opened not his mouth; like a lamb that is led to the slaughter, and like a sheep that before its shearers are silent, so he opened not his mouth.

ISAIAH 53:7

ASK THIS: What's right for you to do today—resist or resist not?

DO THIS: Act rightly with an eye to God's pending judgment.

PRAY THIS: God, may my thoughts, speech, and action reflect your righteousness in light of your judgment.

ESTABLISHED IN PATIENCE

You also, be patient. Establish your hearts,
for the coming of the Lord is at hand.

JAMES 5:8

Most of us know that patience is an output of living a life guided by the Holy Spirit. However, there are also times when biblical writers command us to cooperate with the Spirit's promptings toward patience. James is telling us to give some attention to our impatient emotions by being patient. And we all know (given the world we are living in today) that commanding our fleshy desires to submit to the Holy Spirit may be the needed action. Could today be that day for you? Is today a day when your flesh may want something faster than it appears God is providing? If so, command your flesh to submit to God's Spirit, for the coming of the Lord is at hand.

Take that flesh!

ASK THIS: Is your flesh impatient?

DO THIS: Let God's Spirit, not your spirit, reign in you!

PRAY THIS: God, reign in me with all your power. Bring heaven down and drive the world out of me!

HE'S AT THE DOOR

Do not grumble against one another,
brothers, so that you may not be judged;
behold, the Judge is standing at the door.

JAMES 5:9

One thing's for sure; the judgment that awaits us all has a righteous, holy, and just Judge. His presence begets power and authority, and our meeting with the Judge is imminent. He does not act like the judges, politicians, and leaders of our time who merely grumble against one another, debating endlessly about who is right or wrong. While we love to convince ourselves we are more in the right compared with others, we must confront this truth, *"there is no one righteous, no not one." — Romans 3:10*

Today is the day to be prepared. He's at the door. He's standing at the ready. So believe, be baptized, and be saved.

Whoever believes and is baptized will be saved, but
whoever does not believe will be condemned.

MARK 16:16

ASK THIS: Are you ready?

DO THIS: Believe and be baptized.

PRAY THIS: God, I confess all my unrighteousness. I accept today your grace, mercy, love, and forgiveness. Cleanse me of all unrighteousness. Until your imminent return, I cling to you as the just Judge and follow you as the Lord and Savior of my life. Amen.

IT'S TIME FOR PROPHETS

As an example of suffering and patience, brothers, take the prophets who spoke in the name of the Lord.

JAMES 5:10

We live in a time of suffering: physical, economic, social, and political suffering. This is not real suffering. Real suffering is to suffer for a truly virtuous cause, a cause a high as the Lord himself.

Our time of suffering is here. It's time to speak. We need to speak boldly in the name of the Lord. Do not back down. There is no better suffering than to suffer like the prophets of the old.

ASK THIS: Are you prepared to suffer?

DO THIS: Hold fast to the Word of God.

PRAY THIS: God, I trust you. I am patient. I am willing. Please give me a platform from which to speak and the words to say.

FIND HEALING

Is anyone among you sick? Let him call for the elders of the church, and let them pray over him, anointing him with oil in the name of the Lord.

JAMES 5:14

At some point, we realize that only God can heal. Yet with the advancement of medicine and technology we have come to trust more in human ingenuity than a God who heals. While I deeply appreciate the care and devotion of my friends who are physicians, they are merely humans with human solutions manipulating the body, hoping that it will heal. However, God created us. He is the Great Physician—he possesses healing power.

The simplicity of James' teaching is profound. If you are sick, turn to God. But the way we do it is important. The command is to *"call for the elders of the church."*

There is a divine and supernatural ministry we need today. The narrative of our time is indoctrinating us with its solutions, security, and salvation. We must not let these narratives replace divine and supernatural ministry that is only accomplished by being in the presence of one another and through the power of prayer.

ASK THIS: Do you need healing?

DO THIS: Ask another follower and your church to pray for you.

PRAY THIS: God, deafen my ears to the narratives of this time. Open my ears to the convictions and guidance of your word. And then give me the courage to act in obedience when it looks like foolishness to the world.

THE POWERFUL PRAYERS OF THE RIGHTEOUS

Therefore, confess your sins to one another and pray for one another, that you may be healed. The prayer of a righteous person has great power as it is working.

JAMES 5:16

We live in a twisted world, one that is more rapidly becoming divided by sin. But what we are experiencing can be healed. It is healed through confession and prayer of a righteous person. Brothers acting in rebellion to sin with more sin is not the answer. But a righteous follower can usher in a time of healing. It beings with a confession of sin and prayer. And let this work, for the prayer of the person who is right with God has great power.

ASK THIS: What do you need to confess?

DO THIS: Confess and let someone pray for you. Start a healing movement!

PRAY THIS: God, I confess my sin of selfishness. Heal me. Heal our land.

HOW TO STOP THE PROGRESS OF SIN

My brothers, if anyone among you wanders from the truth and someone brings him back, let him know that whoever brings back a sinner from his wandering will save his soul from death and will cover a multitude of sins.

JAMES 5:19-20

People are wandering. They are wandering because their world has been turned upside down by marriage failures, job losses, sicknesses, addictions, and all kinds of oppression. While it is tragic, it is an opportunity for souls to be brought back from wandering and death. Each of us knows one man that can be brought back from the downward spiral of sin. Today, allow God's Spirit to prompt your mind with a brother's name. Then reach out to him and bring him back—not to your way, but to God, and in so doing cover over a multitude of potential sins.

ASK THIS: Who is someone that comes to mind?

DO THIS: Call, text, or email this person and pray with them.

PRAY THIS: God, bring to mind one name. Give me the courage to call and bring them back.

Will - Wife's mother + dimentia/
parkensens
Jonathan - Struggling with
the what ifs + nephews
Eddie - kids (Gavin) + faith
                    &
                  Austin
Dennis - Donna's health
Keith - depression / meaning

GG	TG
GT	TT